Dots and Spots

by Orlando Frizado

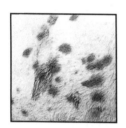 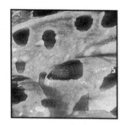  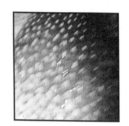

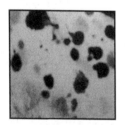 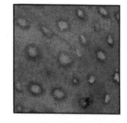 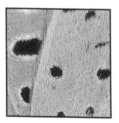

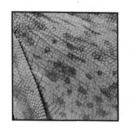  

SCHOLASTIC INC.

New York   Toronto   London   Auckland   Sydney
Mexico City   New Delhi   Hong Kong   Buenos Aires

Dots, dots, dots.
Dots and spots.
Dots run and run.
Dots do not stop.

Dots, dots, dots.
Dots and spots.
Dots flap, flap, flap.
Dots flop.

Dots, dots, dots.
Dots and spots.
Dots hop up.
Dots hop on top.

Dots, dots, dots.
Dots and spots.
Dots tap, tap, tap.
Dots pop out.

Dots, dots, dots.
Dots and spots.
Dots dig and dig.
Dots have fun.

Dots, dots, dots.
Dots and spots.
Dots sit in the sun.
Dots get hot.

Dots, dots, dots.
Dots and spots.
Dots swim, swim, swim.
Dots get wet.

Dots, dots, dots.
Dots and spots.
Dots are not bad.
Dots snap up bugs.

Dots, dots, dots.
Dots and spots.
Dots flit, flit, land.
Dots dip and sip.

12

Dots, dots, dots.
Dots and spots.
Dots nap.
Dots nap a lot!

Photo Credits:
Cover: A&M Shah/Animals Animals; p. 2: Robert Maier/Animals Animals;
p. 3 Ken Cole/Animals Animals; p. 4: James Balog/Stone/Getty Images;
p. 5: MH Sharp/Photo Researchers, Inc.; p. 6: Zig Leszczynski/Animals Animals;
p. 7: Alain Schall/Photo Researchers, Inc.; p. 8: Norbert Wu;
p. 9: Stephen Dalton/Photo Researchers, Inc.;
p. 10: Patti Murray/Animals Animals; p. 11: A&M Shah/Animals Animals

ISBN 0-439-40381-2

1 2 3 4 5 6 7 8 9 10   24   10 09 08 07 06 05 04 03 02